Red Foxes

Victoria Blakemore

For Uncle Clive, with love

Table of Contents

What are Red Foxes?   2

Size   4

Physical Characteristics   6

Habitat   8

Range   10

Diet   12

Communication   16

Movement   18

Red Fox Kits   20

Fox Life   22

Red Foxes as Pets   24

Population   26

Are Foxes Pests?   28

Helping Red Foxes   30

Glossary   34

What Are Red Foxes?

Foxes are mammals. They are members of the canid family. They are related to animals like wolves, dogs, and coyotes.

There are thirty different kinds of foxes. The most common kind of fox is the red fox.

Red foxes have red-orange fur
with a white chest and black
paws.

Size

When fully grown, red foxes are usually between eighteen and thirty-four inches long. Their tail adds another twelve to twenty inches to their length.

Red foxes can weigh between six and twenty-four pounds. Most are around ten pounds.

Male red foxes are usually

larger than female red foxes.

Physical Characteristics

Red foxes have a very thick coat of fur. It helps them to stay warm. They shed their extra fur when the weather is warmer.

They have a long, pointed **snout**. Their sense of smell is very good and helps them to find their prey.

Foxes have a thick, bushy tail that helps them to balance. They also use their tail to cover themselves up and keep warm when it is cold outside.

Habitat

Red foxes live in forests, grasslands, mountains, and deserts. They are sometimes found around farms and neighborhoods.

They are able to **adapt** to living in many different habitats.

Red foxes are found in North America, Europe, Asia, and Australia.

They are often seen in countries
like Russia, Canada, America,
Great Britain, and Norway.

Diet

Foxes are **omnivores**, which means that they eat meat and plants.

Their diet is made up of rodents, rabbits, birds, fish, fruits, and vegetables. They have also been known to get into people's trash.

Foxes sometimes catch more prey than they can eat, then bury the extra to save it for later.

Red foxes have very good hearing. In the winter, it can be harder to find food. They listen for sounds of movement under the snow.

When they hear something move, they pounce and punch through the ice with their paws to catch their prey.

Red foxes catch their prey by
pouncing on it. Other kinds of
foxes pounce on their prey too.

Communication

Foxes use sound, scent, and movement to communicate with each other.

Red foxes may mark their **territory** with their scent. It tells other foxes to stay away. Certain movements, like the flicking of a tail, can be used as a warning.

Red foxes use sounds such as
whines, barks, screams, and
growls.

Movement

Red foxes are able to run at speeds of up to thirty miles per hour. This helps them to catch prey and stay safe from predators.

They are good climbers and can climb over fences to find food. They are not as good at climbing as the gray fox.

Although red foxes can run fast,

they usually only do so for short

distances.

Fox Kits

Foxes have a **litter** of between two and twelve babies. Their babies are called kits.

When they are first born, kits are brown or gray. Their red coat will grow in after about a month.

Both parents take care of kits

until they are old enough to

take care of themselves.

Fox Life

Fox families live in dens that they have dug in the dirt or made in a hollow log. It keeps them safe from predators and warm when it is cold.

A group of foxes is called a skulk. Some foxes live by themselves.

Some red foxes are **nocturnal**.

They are more active at night

and sleep during the day.

Foxes as Pets

Some people have a **domesticated** fox as a pet. Taking care of a pet fox can be difficult. They are not the right pet for everyone.

They need more time outside than most pets and it can be hard to find a vet that can help a fox if it gets sick.

Foxes that are **domesticated**

can have behaviors like dogs.

They can be very **affectionate**.

Population

Red foxes are not

endangered. Their population

in the wild is **stable**. This is

because they are able to

adapt to many different

habitats.

They are trapped for their fur,

meat, and because they are

thought to be pests.

In the wild, foxes usually between two and four years. They may live longer in **captivity**.

Are Red Foxes Pests?

Farmers and ranchers who raise **livestock** such as chickens and turkeys may have problems with red foxes.

The red foxes can catch and eat their **livestock**. They can climb fences and get into many animal pens.

Helping Red Foxes

Red foxes populations are not in trouble, but there are still ways they can be helped.

Many of these ways involve keeping **livestock** safe from red foxes. If they are not able to catch people's **livestock**, they may not be trapped and killed as often.

30

Fences can be used to keep animals safe from foxes, but only if they have a cover over the top. Noise makers and lights can also be used to scare foxes away.

The goal of these methods is to keep foxes away from **livestock** without needing to trap or kill them.

Glossary

Adapt: to change, adjust, or become used to

Affectionate: showing love

Captivity: when animals are kept by people, not in the wild

Domesticated: an animal that is used to living with humans, tame

Endangered: at risk of becoming extinct

Litter: a group of animals born at the same time

Livestock: animals raised and kept on a farm or ranch

Nocturnal: animals that are active at night

Omnivore: an animal that eats meat and plants

Snout: the front part of an animals face that sticks out, the nose and mouth area

Stable: unchanging

Territory: an area of land that an animal claims as its own

About the Author

Victoria Blakemore is a first grade

teacher in Southwest Florida with a

passion for reading.

You can visit her at

www.elementaryexplorers.com

Also in This Series

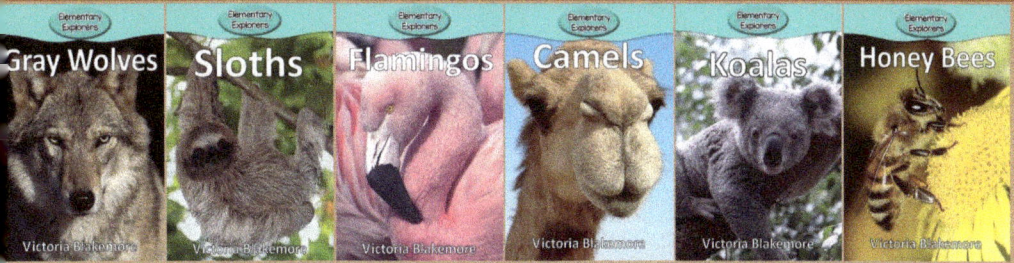

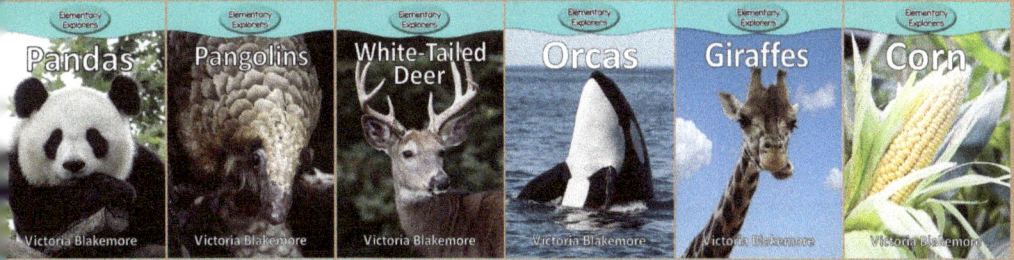

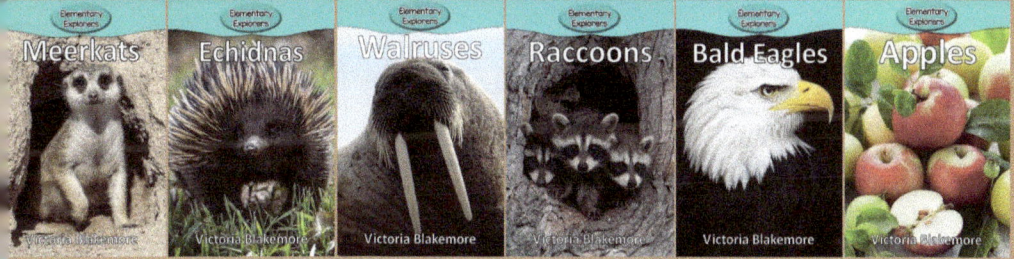

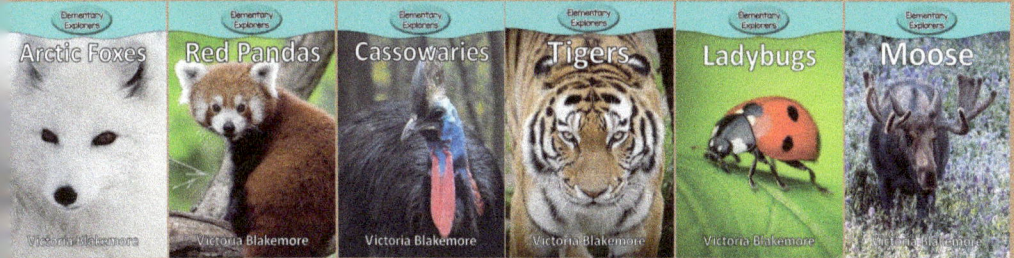

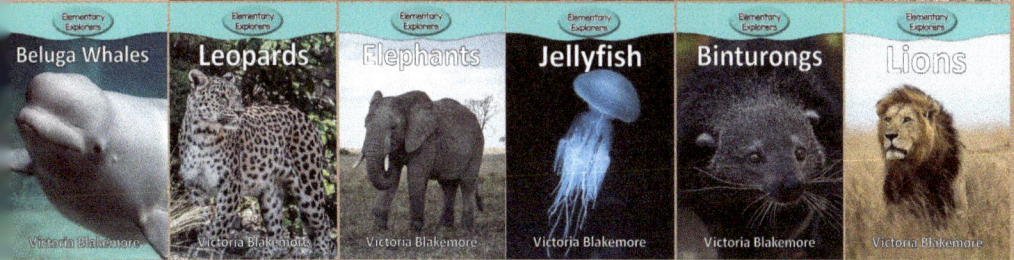

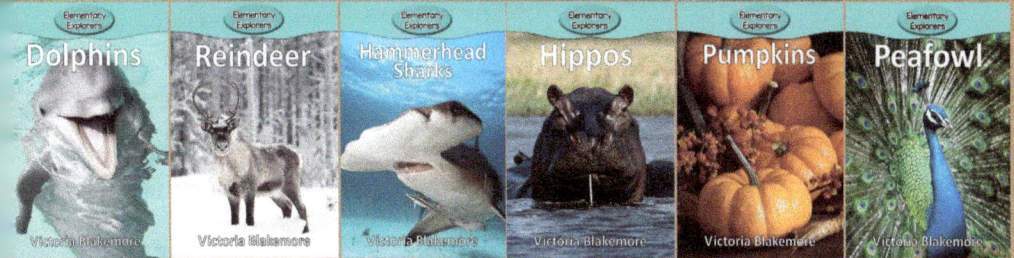

Gray Wolves

Sloths

Flamingos

Camels

Koalas

Honey Bees

Pandas

Pangolins

White-Tailed Deer

Orcas

Giraffes

Corn

Meerkats

Echidnas

Walruses

Raccoons

Bald Eagles

Apples

Arctic Foxes

Red Pandas

Cassowaries

Tigers

Ladybugs

Moose

Beluga Whales

Leopards

Elephants

Jellyfish

Binturongs

Lions

Dolphins

Reindeer

Hammerhead Sharks

Hippos

Pumpkins

Peafowl

Also in This Series

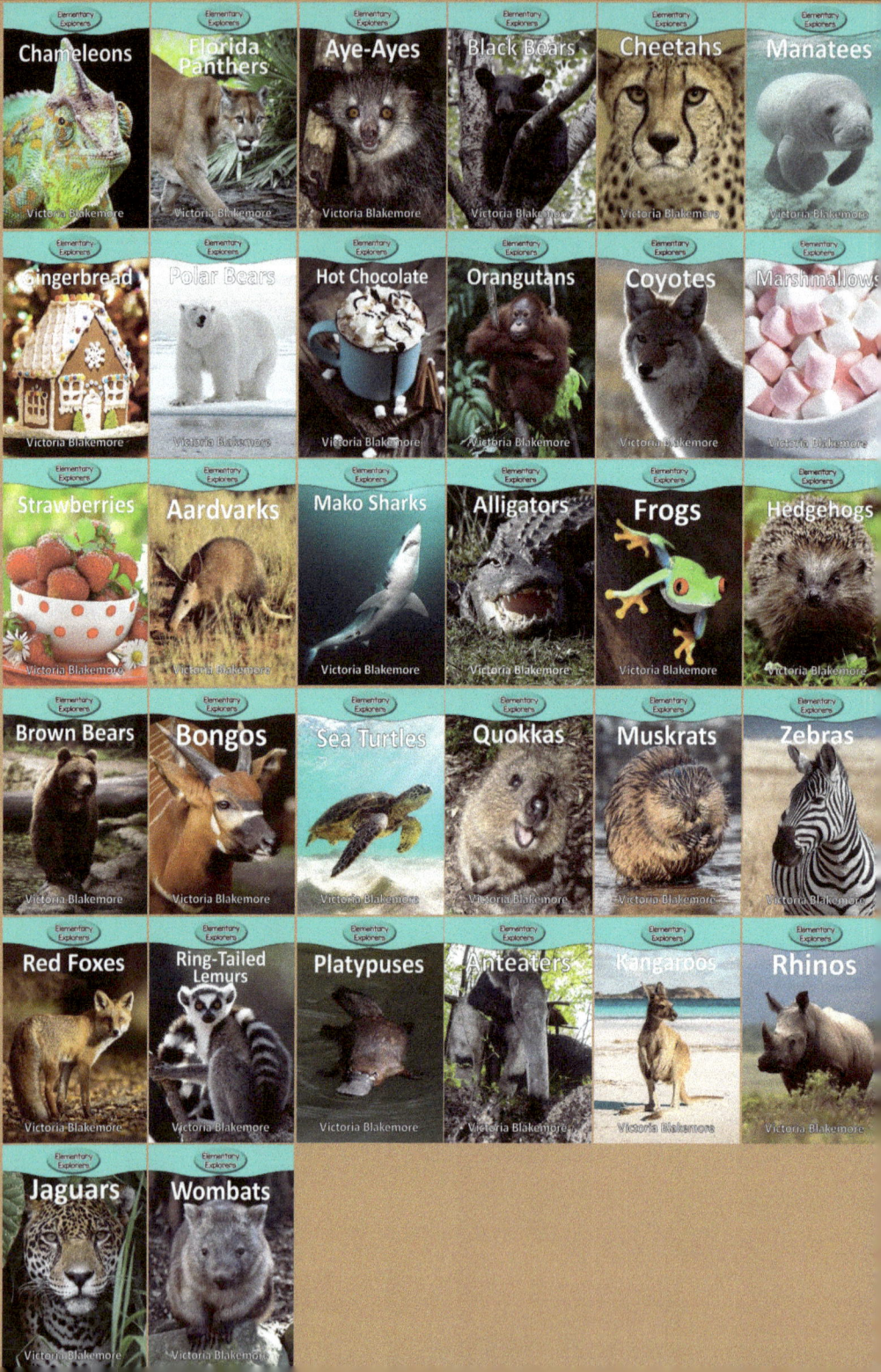

Elementary Explorers — Chameleons — Victoria Blakemore

Elementary Explorers — Florida Panthers — Victoria Blakemore

Elementary Explorers — Aye-Ayes — Victoria Blakemore

Elementary Explorers — Black Bears — Victoria Blakemore

Elementary Explorers — Cheetahs — Victoria Blakemore

Elementary Explorers — Manatees — Victoria Blakemore

Elementary Explorers — Gingerbread — Victoria Blakemore

Elementary Explorers — Polar Bears — Victoria Blakemore

Elementary Explorers — Hot Chocolate — Victoria Blakemore

Elementary Explorers — Orangutans — Victoria Blakemore

Elementary Explorers — Coyotes — Victoria Blakemore

Elementary Explorers — Marshmallows — Victoria Blakemore

Elementary Explorers — Strawberries — Victoria Blakemore

Elementary Explorers — Aardvarks — Victoria Blakemore

Elementary Explorers — Mako Sharks — Victoria Blakemore

Elementary Explorers — Alligators — Victoria Blakemore

Elementary Explorers — Frogs — Victoria Blakemore

Elementary Explorers — Hedgehogs — Victoria Blakemore

Elementary Explorers — Brown Bears — Victoria Blakemore

Elementary Explorers — Bongos — Victoria Blakemore

Elementary Explorers — Sea Turtles — Victoria Blakemore

Elementary Explorers — Quokkas — Victoria Blakemore

Elementary Explorers — Muskrats — Victoria Blakemore

Elementary Explorers — Zebras — Victoria Blakemore

Elementary Explorers — Red Foxes — Victoria Blakemore

Elementary Explorers — Ring-Tailed Lemurs — Victoria Blakemore

Elementary Explorers — Platypuses — Victoria Blakemore

Elementary Explorers — Anteaters — Victoria Blakemore

Elementary Explorers — Kangaroos — Victoria Blakemore

Elementary Explorers — Rhinos — Victoria Blakemore

Elementary Explorers — Jaguars — Victoria Blakemore

Elementary Explorers — Wombats — Victoria Blakemore

www.ingramcontent.com/pod-product-compliance
Lightning Source LLC
Chambersburg PA
CBHW051253020426
42333CB00025B/3190